Francis Frith's
ENGLISH CASTLES

PHOTOGRAPHIC MEMORIES

Francis Frith's
ENGLISH CASTLES

◆

Clive Hardy

First published in the United Kingdom in 1999 by
Frith Book Company Ltd

Hardback Edition 1999
ISBN 1-85937-078-0

Paperback Edition 2001
ISBN 1-85937-434-4

Reprinted in Paperback 2005

British Library Cataloguing in Publication Data

Francis Frith's English Castles
Clive Hardy

Frith Book Company Ltd
Frith's Barn, Teffont,
Salisbury, Wiltshire SP3 5QP
Tel: +44 (0) 1722 716 376
Email: info@francisfrith.co.uk
www.francisfrith.co.uk

Cover Image: **WINDSOR, THE CASTLE, HENRY VIII GATE 1914** 66985t

The colour-tinting is for illustrative purposes only, and is not intended to be historically accurate

Printed and bound in Great Britain

AS WITH ANY HISTORICAL DATABASE THE FRITH ARCHIVE IS CONSTANTLY BEING CORRECTED AND IMPROVED
AND THE PUBLISHERS WOULD WELCOME INFORMATION ON OMISSIONS OR INACCURACIES

CONTENTS

FRANCIS FRITH: *Victorian Pioneer*

FRANCIS FRITH, Victorian founder of the world-famous photographic archive, was a complex and multitudinous man. A devout Quaker and a highly successful Victorian businessman, he was both philosophical by nature and pioneering in outlook.

By 1855 Francis Frith had already established a wholesale grocery business in Liverpool, and sold it for the astonishing sum of £200,000, which is the equivalent today of over £15,000,000. Now a very rich man, he was able to indulge his passion for travel. As a child he had pored over travel books written by early explorers, and his fancy and imagination had been stirred by family holidays to the sublime mountain regions of Wales and Scotland. 'What lands of spirit-stirring and enriching scenes and places!' he had written. He was to return to these scenes of grandeur in later years to 'recapture the thousands of vivid and tender memories', but with a different purpose. Now in his thirties, and captivated by the new science of photography, Frith set out on a series of pioneering journeys to the Nile regions that occupied him from 1856 until 1860.

INTRIGUE AND ADVENTURE

He took with him on his travels a specially-designed wicker carriage that acted as both dark-room and sleeping chamber. These far-flung journeys were packed with intrigue and adventure. In his life story, written when he was sixty-three, Frith tells of being held captive by bandits, and of fighting 'an awful midnight battle to the very point of surrender with a deadly pack of hungry, wild dogs'. Sporting flowing Arab costume, Frith arrived at Akaba by camel sixty years before Lawrence, where he encountered 'desert princes and rival sheikhs, blazing with jewel-hilted swords'.

During these extraordinary adventures he was assiduously exploring the desert regions bordering the Nile and patiently recording the antiquities and peoples with his camera. He was the first photographer to venture beyond the sixth cataract. Africa was still the mysterious 'Dark Continent', and Stanley and Livingstone's historic meeting was a decade into the future. The conditions for picture taking confound belief. He laboured for hours in his wicker dark-room in the sweltering heat of the desert, while the volatile chemicals fizzed dangerously in their trays. Often he was forced to work in remote tombs and caves where conditions were cooler. Back in London he exhibited his photographs and was 'rapturously cheered' by members of the Royal Society. His reputation as a photographer was made overnight. An eminent modern historian has likened their impact on the population of the time to that on our own generation of the first photographs taken on the surface of the moon.

VENTURE OF A LIFE-TIME

Characteristically, Frith quickly spotted the opportunity to create a new business as a specialist publisher of photographs. He lived in an era of immense and sometimes violent change. For the poor in the early part of Victoria's reign work was a drudge and the hours long, and people had precious little free time to enjoy themselves.

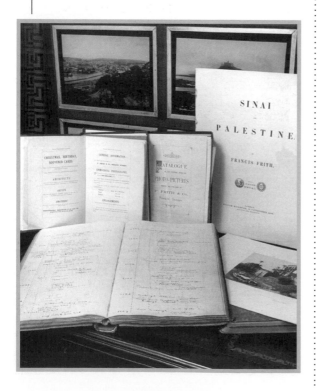

Most had no transport other than a cart or gig at their disposal, and had not travelled far beyond the boundaries of their own town or village. However, by the 1870s, the railways had threaded their way across the country, and Bank Holidays and half-day Saturdays had been made obligatory by Act of Parliament. All of a sudden the ordinary working man and his family were able to enjoy days out and see a little more of the world.

With characteristic business acumen, Francis Frith foresaw that these new tourists would enjoy having souvenirs to commemorate their days out. In 1860 he married Mary Ann Rosling and set out with the intention of photographing every city, town and village in Britain. For the next thirty years he travelled the country by train and by pony and trap, producing fine photographs of seaside resorts and beauty spots that were keenly bought by millions of Victorians. These prints were painstakingly pasted into family albums and pored over during the dark nights of winter, rekindling precious memories of summer excursions.

THE RISE OF FRITH & CO

Frith's studio was soon supplying retail shops all over the country. To meet the demand he gathered about him a small team of photographers, and published the work of independent artist-photographers of the calibre of Roger Fenton and Francis Bedford. In order to gain some understanding of the scale of Frith's business one only has to look at the catalogue issued by Frith & Co in 1886: it runs to some 670 pages, listing not

only many thousands of views of the British Isles but also many photographs of most European countries, and China, Japan, the USA and Canada – note the sample page shown above from the hand-written *Frith & Co* ledgers detailing pictures taken. By 1890 Frith had created the greatest specialist photographic publishing company in the world, with over 2,000 outlets – more than the combined number that Boots and WH Smith have today! The picture on the right shows the *Frith & Co* display board at Ingleton in the Yorkshire Dales (left of window). Beautifully constructed with a mahogany frame and gilt inserts, it could display up to a dozen local scenes.

POSTCARD BONANZA

The ever-popular holiday postcard we know today took many years to develop. In 1870 the Post Office issued the first plain cards, with a pre-printed stamp on one face. In 1894 they allowed other publishers' cards to be sent through the mail with an attached adhesive halfpenny stamp. Demand grew rapidly, and in 1895 a new size of postcard was permitted called the court card, but there was little room for illustration. In 1899, a year after Frith's death, a new card measuring 5.5 x 3.5 inches became the standard format, but it was not until 1902 that the divided back came into being, with address and message on one face and a full-size illustration on the other. *Frith & Co* were in the vanguard of postcard development, and Frith's sons Eustace and Cyril continued their father's monumental task, expanding the number of views offered to the public and recording more and more places in Britain, as the coasts and countryside were opened up to mass travel.

Francis Frith died in 1898 at his villa in Cannes, his great project still growing. The archive he created continued in business for another seventy years. By 1970 it contained over a third of a million pictures of 7,000 cities, towns and villages. The massive photographic record Frith has left to us stands as a living monument to a special and very remarkable man.

Frith's Archive: *A Unique Legacy*

FRANCIS FRITH'S legacy to us today is of immense significance and value, for the magnificent archive of evocative photographs he created provides a unique record of change in 7,000 cities, towns and villages throughout Britain over a century and more. Frith and his fellow studio photographers revisited locations many times down the years to update their views, compiling for us an enthralling and colourful pageant of British life and character.

We tend to think of Frith's sepia views of Britain as nostalgic, for most of us use them to conjure up memories of places in our own lives with which we have family associations. It often makes us forget that to Francis Frith they were records of daily life as it was actually being lived in the cities, towns and villages of his day. The Victorian age was one of great and often bewildering change for ordinary people, and though the pictures evoke an impression of slower times, life was as busy and hectic as it is today.

We are fortunate that Frith was a photographer of the people, dedicated to recording the minutiae of everyday life. For it is this sheer wealth of visual data, the painstaking chronicle of changes in dress, transport, street layouts, buildings, housing, engineering and landscape that captivates us so much today. His remarkable images offer us a powerful link with the past and with the lives of our ancestors.

TODAY'S TECHNOLOGY

Computers have now made it possible for Frith's many thousands of images to be accessed almost instantly. In the Frith archive today, each photograph is carefully 'digitised' then stored on a CD Rom. Frith archivists can locate a single photograph amongst thousands within seconds. Views can be catalogued and sorted under a variety of categories of place and content to the immediate benefit of researchers. Inexpensive reference prints can be created for them at the touch of a mouse button, and a wide range of books and other printed materials assembled and published for a wider, more general readership - in the next twelve months over a hundred Frith local history titles will be published! The

See Frith at www. francisfrith.co.uk

10

day-to-day workings of the archive are very different from how they were in Francis Frith's time: imagine the herculean task of sorting through eleven tons of glass negatives as Frith had to do to locate a particular sequence of pictures! Yet the archive still prides itself on maintaining the same high standards of excellence laid down by Francis Frith, including the painstaking cataloguing and indexing of every view.

It is curious to reflect on how the internet now allows researchers in America and elsewhere greater instant access to the archive than Frith himself ever enjoyed. Many thousands of individual views can be called up on screen within seconds on one of the Frith internet sites, enabling people living continents away to revisit the streets of their ancestral home town, or view places in Britain where they have enjoyed holidays. Many overseas researchers welcome the chance to view special theme selections, such as transport, sports, costume and ancient monuments.

We are certain that Francis Frith would have heartily approved of these modern developments, for he himself was always working at the very limits of Victorian photographic technology.

THE VALUE OF THE ARCHIVE TODAY

Because of the benefits brought by the computer, Frith's images are increasingly studied by social historians, by researchers into genealogy and ancestory, by architects, town planners, and by teachers and school-children involved in local history projects. In addition, the archive offers every one of us a unique opportunity to examine the places where we and our families have lived and worked down the years. Immensely successful in Frith's own era, the archive is now, a century and more on, entering a new phase of popularity.

THE PAST IN TUNE WITH THE FUTURE

Historians consider the Francis Frith Collection to be of prime national importance. It is the only archive of its kind remaining in private ownership and has been valued at a million pounds. However, this figure is now rapidly increasing as digital technology enables more and more people around the world to enjoy its benefits.

Francis Frith's archive is now housed in an historic timber barn in the beautiful village of Teffont in Wiltshire. Its founder would not recognize the archive office as it is today. In place of the many thousands of dusty boxes containing glass plate negatives and an all-pervading odour of photographic chemicals, there are now ranks of computer screens. He would be amazed to watch his images travelling round the world at unimaginable speeds through network and internet lines.

The archive's future is both bright and exciting. Francis Frith, with his unshakeable belief in making photographs available to the greatest number of people, would undoubtedly approve of what is being done today with his lifetime's work. His photographs, depicting our shared past, are now bringing pleasure and enlightenment to millions around the world a century and more after his death.

ENGLISH CASTLES – *An Introduction*

THE NORMAN INHERITANCE

THE WORD CASTLE conjures up different things to different people - knights in armour, damsels in distress, robber barons, Robin Hood and the Sheriff of Nottingham and so on. But the castle was something unique: it was a fortified residence from which a lord could exert control over the surrounding area. The earliest castles were in Normandy. Duke Richard I (942-996) built a stone tower at Rouen and fortified a palace at Bayeux. Richard II (996-1026) and Richard III (1026-27) raised castles at Tillieres, Falaise, Le Homme, Cherbourg and Brix. But it would be under Duke William that the association of castles, lordship, and control, would truly manifest itself and be expanded upon. In 1047 William built a castle at Caen which enabled him to exercise political, social and military control over lower Normandy. In that same year he defeated rebel Norman lords at Val-les-Dunes and ordered their castles destroyed.

There were a handful of castles in England before the Conquest, built by Norman lords who had settled in the country by the invita-tion of Edward the Confessor. The known ones were at Hereford, Ewyas Harold, and Richard's Castle. Less certain in date are the castle at Clavering in Essex and Dover Castle. Richard's Castle was a motte and bailey type, built in Herefordshire by Richard FitzScrob before 1051; it was successfully held by him during the anti-Norman rising led by Godwin, Earl of Wessex. Dover Castle could be early in date because chroniclers relate that Harold promised it to William when he swore his oath in 1064. Though evidence is lacking, a castle might have existed; but Harold could have been referring to an Anglo-Saxon fortifica-tion.

Following the Norman invasion, a consid-erable number of motte and bailey castles with wooden towers and palisades were thrown up in order to assert control over the country. Many of these would soon be aban-doned as feudal authority took control; others would become far more permanent, their wooden structures replaced by ones of stone. Within a short space of time the knight and the castle would become the embodiment of warfare in the feudal period. The ethos of the times was such that besieging a castle, and the etiquette associated with it, would be just as important as fighting a pitched battle.

By the late 12th century the building of stone castles dominated the royal policies of Henry II, Richard I and King John. Sums spent varied from one castle to another: the keep at Dover cost Henry II £4000, though overall he spent around £7000 on Dover. The Tower of London cost £2400, yet only £50 a year was spent on Hereford and Gloucester castles.

By around 1200, any lord obtaining a licence to crenellate not only had the construction costs to find (and these could be considerable), but would have to commit £100 to £150 a year to cover running costs. Edward I spent a fortune on building six major castles and strengthening others during his wars against the Welsh. At the lower end of his expenses, £318 was spent upgrading the defences at Criccieth; Harlech, however, took six years and £8000 to build, and Flint a little over nine years and £7000. Beaumaris cost £14500, and the castle and town walls at Caernavon together cost £19900. With several castles under construction at once, Edward recruited workers from throughout England. In 1277 almost 3000 men assembled at Chester, where they were allocated to works at Flint, Rhuddlan and elsewhere. In addition to his own enthusiastic building programme, Edward actively encouraged his loyal barons such as Payn de Chaworth to rebuild their own fortresses, often through subsidies from the Crown.

The stakes were always high for the big spenders of Medieval England, whether they were noble or royal. At some time during April 1327 the deposed Edward II was brought to Berkeley Castle following his arrest and detainment at Kenilworth. Edward's weak rule and a reliance on favourites rather than experienced men had alienated the barons; even his queen Isabella went for a time into exile. Isabella became the mistress of the exiled baron Roger Mortimer, and in 1326 they led an army to England. The outcome of this was the deposing of Edward. But Edward's continuing survival posed a serious threat to Isabella and her plan to put her son on the throne; Edward had to go. His custodian, the third Baron Berkeley, was forced

to surrender both castle and royal prisoner to John, Lord Maltrevers, who then set about trying to kill the king. It was attempted through deprivation, and also by throwing rotting animal corpses into a pit in the corner of Edward's room in the hope that he would either be asphyxiated or contract something very nasty and terminal. Edward did neither: he was made of stronger stuff. His death had

Nibley Green in 1470: the rival factions met in armed combat, and Berkeley became the scene of the last private pitched battle on English soil.

William Lord Hastings, Chamberlain of the Royal Household, Master of the Mint, Chamberlain of North Wales, Receiver of the revenue of the Duchy of Cornwall, Lieutenant of Calais, Knight of the Garter, was another

to appear to be from natural causes, and it was officially announced as such on 22nd September 1327. When Jean Froissart visited Berkeley in 1366, he was told that Edward had been murdered. Death was caused by 'a hoote brooche putte thro the secret place posteri-alle'. The thinking behind shoving a red hot poker up the king's bottom was so as not to leave any outward signs of physical violence. There were, of course, connotations connected with Edward's known homosexual practices and his favourite Piers Gaveston.

Thomas, third Lord Berkeley had remodelled the castle between 1340-50; when he died his daughter was outraged that her inheritance must go to a nephew. She sued, and thus began a family feud destined to last two hundred years. Things came to a head on

character to whom riches did not bring happiness. Life for Lord Hastings must have looked good. He had received his licence to crenellate in 1472, and in 1480 he began building Kirby Muxloe Castle, an early example of the use of brick. The entrance was across a moat defended by a drawbridge, portcullis and two pairs of folding doors. The gatehouse and each of the four corner towers were equipped with loops for handguns, but even so Kirby Muxloe was intended by his lordship as a social statement rather than a military installation. In the early summer of 1483, William Lord Hastings' career came to a swift end. It was during a meeting that Hastings was seized by Richard of Gloucester, tried, condemned and probably executed on the spot. The event was dramatised by

Shakespeare in 'Richard III': 'Thou art a traitor:- Off with his head! -now, by Saint Paul, I swear I will not dine until I see the same.' After Hastings' execution, his widow continued some work on the castle, but this might have been limited to finishing the west tower.

HENRY VIII'S COAST DEFENCE CASTLES

Henry VIII was desperate for a male heir. After eighteen years of marriage, he decided to divorce his wife Catherine of Aragon and marry Anne Bullen. Henry needed the permission of both the Pope and the Holy Roman Emperor Charles V - who just happened to be Catherine's nephew. Their refusal to agree to the divorce led Henry to set himself up as the head of the Church in England; an action that would see men like Sir Thomas More executed, and the Dissolution of the monasteries. By 1538, Pope Paul III was actively preaching for a crusade against England; he hoped that France and Spain would forget their differences and join forces in an invasion that would see England returned to Papal authority.

A direct result of this threat was a strengthening of the Royal Navy and the construction of a series of coast defence batteries to protect potential anchorages. There were five castles protecting the Thames between Tilbury and Gravesend; the Sandown, Deal and Walmer chain covering the Downs; and other castles at Dover, Southampton, Portland, the Isle of Wight, Fowey and Falmouth. The castles at the Kentish end of the line were built in a little over eighteen months, but those in Cornwall were not completed until 1545-50. Though often called castles, many of the buildings were in fact defended artillery forts under the command of a governor or master-gunner, and as such are not castles in the true definition of the word.

Deal Castle was the largest of Henry's coastal artillery forts. Built c1538-40, it was of a revolutionary design comprising a circular central keep and six lower semi-circular bastions. Around this was a six-lobed curtain wall and a wide dry moat. The castle was provided with long-range guns for use against enemy shipping, and with handguns for close all-round defence.

Pendennis and St Mawes castles were built 1540-50 to guard the Carrick Roads. An inventory for 1547 gives Pendennis as mounting twenty-six guns, mostly wrought-iron breech loaders; additional firepower was provided by twelve stand guns (hackbuts), forty bows and ninety-six sheaves of arrows. Across the Carrick Roads St Mawes, which is sited on lower ground than Pendennis, mounted nineteen guns.

CASTLES AND THE ENGLISH CIVIL WAR

Some castles, such as Conisbrough and Richmond, played no part at all in the English Civil War, while others played significant roles; it was at Nottingham Castle on 22 August 1642 that Charles I raised the royal standard, an act which put both sides on a collision course - instead of talking, men now reached for their swords. It was to Carisbrooke Castle on the Isle of Wight that Charles I fled from Hampton Court. It was here that he effectively became a prisoner of the Parliament until the autumn of 1648, before his removal to Hurst Castle and then to Windsor. Many castles would be the scene of sieges, and some would change hands on more than one occasion; others would be held throughout the war for one side or the other.

On the outbreak of hostilities, Donnington Castle in Berkshire was owned by John Packer, a supporter of the Parliament. However, his castle was seized by Royalists, and fortified on the latest Italian practice with sharp-angled bastions to give maximum cover to the garrison whilst at the same time exposing any assaulting force maximum fire from the defenders. As the castle dominated an important road junction (where the London to Bath and Southampton to Northampton roads met), Parliament considered that the sooner it was taken or neutralised the better.

On 31 July 1644, Lieutenant-General Middleton's troops attacked, but suffered heavy casualties; it was decided to put Donnington under siege. Twenty months of bombardment were answered with retaliatory sorties by the garrison, in which stores and weapons were captured. The siege was raised on two occasions by Charles I himself, and it was on the first of these that the King knight-ed Colonel John Boys, the castle's commander. One interesting story from the siege concerns the castle well: the Parliamentary commander sent word to Boys that the well had been poisoned, and a truce was observed whilst the castle garrison cleaned it out. Taking Donnington became a matter of pride for the Parliamentarians; a massive £6600 was voted for the task, and at least one heavy calibre 15-inch mortar was brought in. Though the castle was in ruins, Boys still managed to hold out. The King raised the siege for the second time on 9 November 1644, but only to collect the treasure and cannon he had left there after the second battle of Newbury. Sir John Boys held Donnington throughout the war, finally surrendering with the full honours of war. After the war the castle, or rather what was left of it, was handed back to John Packer, who then built Donnington Castle House.

During the Civil War, both Pendennis and St Mawes castles were held for the king; a base was established for use by ships bringing much needed supplies, arms and ammunition from the Continent. Pendennis also had its share of royal visitors. In 1644 Queen Henrietta Maria stayed at least one night in

the castle en route to France, and in February 1646 Prince Charles sailed from here for the Isles of Scilly after being ordered by the King to leave England. As Parliamentarian forces continued to gain ground, Royalist troops driven westward headed for Pendennis and St Mawes, where a stand would be made. St Mawes, however, was surrendered on 12 March 1646 by its commanding officer Hannibal Bonython without a shot being fired. Bonython was no fool: he made the right decision, given that St Mawes was overlooked to landward by high ground. Over at Pendennis, John Arundell of Trerice, with a thousand troops under his command, and enough stores and ammunition to last six weeks, prepared for a long siege. Though cut off on land by the forces of Colonel Fortesque and Hammon, and from the seaward by a naval blockade, Arundell in fact held out for nearly six months; he was only compelled to surrender by the plight of his men, many of whom were ill from the effects of starvation. Pendennis surrendered on 17 August, just two days before Raglan Castle, the last garrison to fly the king's standard. In acknowledgement of their stand, the Parliamentarians granted the garrison the full honours of war: to march out of Pendennis with 'drums beating, colours flying, trumpets sounding'.

When the Civil War started, Farnham Castle in Surrey was held by a Parliamentarian garrison, but it was later abandoned and taken over by Royalists under Sir John Denham. Sir John's hold lasted a month at most, for on 1 December 1642 Sir William Waller's troops blew in the gates and took the castle by storm. Parliament ordered Farnham to be slighted, but Sir William Waller used it

as his base for operations. By the end of November 1643 Waller had concentrated at Farnham a force estimated to have been 8000 strong for an attempt to take Winchester. On 5 December news reached Waller that a large force of Royalists had left Oxford intent on intercepting him, whereupon he struck out for his secondary target, Basing House. Waller had been besieging Basing for a little over a week when news came that Hopton was advancing towards him from Andover. Waller retired on Farnham, and the castle's defences were improved. Hopton tried to lure Waller out to fight, but some of his forces got a little too close to the Parliamentarian artillery and were dispersed by gunfire. Waller used Farnham as a base for further attacks on Basing and Arundel Castle, and came here after his victory at Cheriton in April 1644.

CASTLE OR COUNTRY HOUSE?

From the 16th century the nobility of England began building non-fortified residences, and the age of the castle in its true form was coming to an end. Between 1750 and 1766 Alnwick Castle, one of the most important fortresses in the north, was extensively refurbished by Robert Adam to create a ducal residence. It was during this period that the carved stone figures were put up on the gatehouse (see photograph No A223010). In 1854, the fourth Duke of Northumberland added the Prudhoe Tower to give the castle a more imposing air. Many castles underwent a similar transformation to that of Alnwick. Some, like Brancepeth, were virtually demolished and rebuilt, complete with Norman style gatehouses and keeps; others were transformed into Gothic or Jacobean residences. There was, of course, a spate of new castle building, including Bude Castle, Willersley Castle, and Ringwood Castle, and though they were adorned with battlements and towers, they were in fact residences with no military value: the country house had taken over the castle's role as the main residence of the aristocracy and ruling class.

Royal castles underwent similar transformations, and vast amounts were lavished on places like Windsor. Jeffrey Wyatt, a member of a famous 19th-century architectural dynasty, changed his name to Wyatville after being selected to design new royal apartments in the east and south ranges at Windsor Castle. He had already established a reputation for his work on country houses, but Windsor was without doubt to be his signature piece. The brief was drawn up in 1824, with a budget of £150,000. In addition to the new royal apartments, the remodelling was to include the creation of the Grand Corridor, the new King George IV Gateway, additional servants' accommodation, and, perhaps the most difficult of all, the raising in height of the 12th-century Round Tower. In order to double the height of the tower, Wyatville had to devise a method of thickening the walls of the original structure to support the additional weight. By 1826, costs were escalating, and the commissioners added an extra £100,000 to the budget. Forced to give an account as to why the costs were rocketing, Wyatville explained that a considerable number of rotten timbers and structural defects had come to light, all of which had to be rectified. The true extent of this work only became apparent during the rebuilding work following the fire of 1992. By the time Wyatville died, over £800,000 had been spent on Windsor. He was succeeded by Edward Blore, who carried on the great work and made numerous alterations for Queen Victoria.

GLOSSARY OF TERMS

Bailey: defended courtyard or ward of a castle.

Barbican: gated outer work, usually separated by a drawbridge from the main gate of the castle.

Bastion: a work at an artillery fortification that allows defenders to fire along the flanks of the fortification.

Crenellation: licence to crenellate and raise a fortified building.

Curtain: wall enclosing a bailey, ward or courtyard.

Keep: the great tower of a castle, also known as a donjon.

Machicolation: openings in the floor of a projecting parapet that allowed the defenders to drop missiles upon the heads of attackers.

Motte: mound on which castle was built; usually artificial.

Murder holes: openings in ceilings through which attackers could be shot at.

Portcullis: heavy grille made of wood and/or iron protecting an entrance. It was raised or lowered by winches in the gatehouse.

Ringwork: circular or oval shaped defensive bank and ditch surrounding a hall.

HOLY ISLAND c1955 H348112
A Tudor fort sitting on top of Beblowe Crag, Lindisfarne was raised for defence against the Scots. Construction began in 1542 and was completed by 1550, using stone salvaged from the Benedictine priory. The only action the castle ever saw was when it was 'captured' from its garrison of just seven men by two Jacobites; they managed to fly their flag for a few hours before they were eventually thrown out. The castle was demilitarised in 1819, and in 1902 it was converted into a private residence for Edward Hudson by Sir Edwin Lutyens.

BAMBURGH CASTLE c1950 B547021B

A fortified site since the 6th century, the Norman castle at Bamburgh was besieged in 1095 by William II. Unable to take the fortress from Robert de Mowbray, third Earl of Northumberland, William headed south, leaving the prosecution of the siege to others. Mowbray attempted to escape, but was captured. His wife only surrendered Bamburgh after her husband had been paraded before the walls under threat of being blinded. Bamburgh holds the distinction of being the first castle to be breached by gunfire, when forces loyal to Edward IV deployed two large cannon. However, the garrison was already on the point of surrendering, having eaten the last of their horses.

ALNWICK CASTLE GATEHOUSE c1955 A223010
The 11th-century castle was extended by the Percy family after they bought it in 1309. The shell keep was rebuilt by Henry de Percy, and the second Earl is thought to have built the barbican and gatehouse around 1440. We can see here that two square towers flank the archway; these are in turn supported by a pair of octagonal towers. Between the two sets of towers there was once a moat spanned by a drawbridge.

BELSAY CASTLE c1955 B554001
The original castle consisted of a three-storey tower with a large room on each floor, with other rooms off the projections. The tower parapet is equipped with machiolations. Belsay was built in the early 14th century, though it is not known if it was protected by a curtain wall or if there were any other buildings. The attached manor house was erected in 1614.

NEWCASTLE UPON TYNE CASTLE 1901 N16022
In 1812 the castle was bought by the Corporation, and it was after this date that
the corner turrets and battlements were added to the keep. Also in the picture
is the Black Gate, originally constructed in 1247 when the castle's defences
were upgraded. The house on the top of the gate is a much later addition.

RABY CASTLE c1955 S292006

RABY CASTLE c1955

Standing in 270 acres of parkland, Raby Castle was the seat of the Neville family for two hundred years. It was at Raby in 1569 that the Rising of the North was planned: the intention was to place Mary, Queen of Scots on the throne of England in place of Elizabeth Tudor. The plot failed, and Raby was forfeited to the Crown. It later came into the possession of the Vane family, though it was temporarily lost by them to the Royalists during the English Civil War following a surprise attack. Not to be outdone, Sir George Vane managed to retake Raby and hold on to it, despite it being besieged in 1648.

BISHOP AUCKLAND CASTLE 1892

Begun as a manor house, Bishop Auckland was castellated around 1300, though much of the building shown here dates from the extensive alterations carried out in the 17th and 18th centuries. The former banqueting hall was converted by Bishop Cosin into the chapel of St Peter during the 1660s after the original had been demolished to make way for a mansion.

BISHOP AUCKLAND CASTLE 1892 30706

DURHAM CASTLE 1892 30759
Work on the original castle began in 1072: it was the official residence of the bishops of Durham. The keep is 14th century, though it was rebuilt in 1840 to house students following the creation of Durham University in 1832. The castle was turned into a university college a few years later.

LUMLEY CASTLE 1892 30720
Sir Robert Lumley was granted licences to crenellate in 1389 and 1392, making Lumley, along with Raby, one of County Durham's two late 14th-century castles. Each of the four square corner towers is topped off with octagonal machicolated turrets, from which unpleasant things could be dropped upon the heads of unwelcome visitors. The turreted and machicolated gatehouse on the east side can be seen through the trees.

BRANCEPETH CASTLE 1914 67122
Brancepeth once belonged to the powerful Neville family, but after changing hands several times it was bought in 1796 by a wealthy Sunderland banker, William Russell. It was he and his son who spent a fortune rebuilding the castle from 1817 onwards. Most of the present buildings are 19th century, even the Norman-style gatehouse.

BARNARD CASTLE 1898 41432

The earliest castle here is thought to have been built by
Bernard de Baliol; it consisted of a ringwork with wooden palisading protected by an outer ditch defence. When John Baliol
was crowned King of Scotland in 1292, his English estates,
including Barnard Castle, were declared forfeit to the English
crown. The Bishop of Durham claimed Barnard, and actually
occupied it from 1296 to 1301, when Edward I took it back and
eventually gave it to Robert Clifford. Over the next couple of
hundred years or so the Bishops of Durham disputed ownership
of the castle with whoever was in residence.

SKELTON CASTLE 1891 29207

There was a castle here in the 12th century; the Bruce family were once lords of the manor. The present castle is a battlemented house dating from around 1800, and the seat of the Wharton family. It was the birthplace of Commander Wild, an Antarctic explorer.

MIDDLEHAM CASTLE 1893 33130

The castle was originally a motte and bailey. The stone keep was built in 1170, with the stone curtain walls and improved living quarters being added shortly afterwards. The castle eventually passed into the hands of the Neville family, and in 1471 Richard, Duke of Gloucester, came here to be tutored by the Earl of Warwick. Richard later married Warwick's daughter Anne, and their son Edward was born at Middleham in 1473; he also died here in 1484. Anne died shortly afterwards, and Richard met his end on Bosworth Field in August 1485.

SKIPTON CASTLE 1888 20955

Skipton was held by the de Clifford family for 375 years. During the English Civil War Sir John Mallory and his 300-strong garrison held out against the Parliamentarians for three years. At the end of the siege, the garrison was accorded the honours of war, and the castle was ordered to be slighted so that cannon could no longer be mounted on its towers. Today the castle is restored and fully roofed.

BOLTON CASTLE 1911 63477

The castle was built by Richard, Lord Scrope some eighteen years after being granted a licence to crenellate by Richard II. Though similar to Bodiam Castle in shape, and designed with a well-defended entrance that featured no less than five doorways and a portcullis at either end, Bolton's principal function appears to have been residential; it was one of the first castles to have chimneys. Mary, Queen of Scots was imprisoned here for six months, and the castle was partially dismantled at the end of the English Civil War. The castle was later used by local families, who lived in tenements built within the walls.

RICHMOND CASTLE 1893 32275

The Norman fortress begun by Alan the Red of Brittany in 1071 dominates the entrance to Swaledale. At that time, the border between an England firmly under Norman control and those still willing to fight lay just a few miles to the north. Alan was the son of the Count of Penthievre, and related to the Duke of Brittany, a relationship that often saw the castle declared forfeit to the Crown. On the right of the picture is Scolland's Hall, dating from c1075 and probably the oldest domestic building in Britain. The 12th-century keep is on the north side. The curtain walls are built on a triangular pattern owing to the shape of the site.

SCARBOROUGH CASTLE 1890 23475
The building of Scarborough Castle began around 1135. The
castle was the scene of the first action by the barons against
Edward II. At the time the castle was held by Piers Gaveston,
Edward's despised favourite. The siege was led by the Earl of
Lancaster, but Gaveston held out until forced by starvation into
surrendering. Despite being promised safe conduct, Gaveston
was seized by the Earl of Warwick and summarily beheaded.
The picture shows the approach to the castle, which was by way
of a narrow causeway, and the remains of the keep that once
stood 100ft high with walls 12ft thick.

YORK, CLIFFORD'S TOWER 1955 Y12018

Clifford's Tower was built by Henry III; it occupies the site of William the Conqueror's motte and bailey destroyed by the Danes in 1069. This castle was soon rebuilt, but it was destroyed a second time during the anti-Jewish riots of 1190. Members of the Jewish community who had sought refuge in the castle either died in the flames when it was set alight or were butchered as they attempted to escape.

YORK, THE CASTLE AND FISHERGATE POSTERN c1885 18496

Despite their looks, the walls and towers round York Castle and Clifford's Tower were not medieval. They were designed by Sydney Smith, Rector of Foston, and built in the 1820s after the site had been purchased by the County Committee for use as a gaol.

YORK, THE CASTLE c1885 18493

John Palmer had been held in a cell in this building for four months - the charges related to his wantonly shooting a cock belonging to his landlord - before the authorities discovered that they were in fact holding the notorious highwayman Dick Turpin. Turpin was executed at York on 10 April 1733. To set the record straight, Dick never rode from London to York in a single night; it took him over a year - and not one of his horses was ever named Black Bess.

KNARESBOROUGH CASTLE 1906 55009

A Norman castle was built here by Serlo de Burg, but the ruins we see are from the 14th century. During the reign of King John, Knaresborough served as a royal arsenal for the manufacture of crossbow quarrels. The castle was extensively rebuilt under the lordship of Piers Gaveston, Edward II's favourite and possibly his lover. Richard II was held here before being taken to Pontefract where he was murdered.

CONISBROUGH CASTLE 1895 35318
This great fortress was built by Hamelin Plantagenet, half-brother of Henry II. The round keep is thought to be the first of its type to be built in England; it was designed to be difficult to mine and resistant to attack with a battering ram. The keep is supported by six wedge-shaped buttresses which rise higher than the keep to form turrets. Though the buttresses served no useful purpose in propping up the keep, they did fulfil certain functions. One contained two cisterns for water drawn from a well beneath the keep; another housed an oven; yet another contained an oratory, and another a pigeon loft.

PONTEFRACT CASTLE 1964 P155035
The ruined shell keep in the south-west corner of Pontefract
Castle dates from the mid-13th century, when it was rebuilt in a
polygonal form similar to those at Knaresborough,
Southampton, Roxburgh and Warkworth. During the English
Civil War the castle was held for the King, changing hands once
before being recaptured by the Royalists. It finally fell in 1648
after a siege lasting six months, and orders were issued for it to
be slighted. Demolition took place between March 1649 and
August 1654; some material was salvaged for repairs
to Hull Castle.

PONTEFRACT CASTLE 1964 P155036

An important part of any castle was the kitchen area and its associated service rooms. These were often built on stone-vaulted floors as a precaution against fire, as can be seen at Castle Rising, and most kitchens boasted more than one oven. The butchery of animals for the pot usually took place in the outer ward: excavations at Porchester revealed that animals were specifically bred for their flesh, rather than being killed and eaten after their milk-producing, egg-laying, or cart-pulling days were over

PONTEFRACT CASTLE 1964 P155030

Pontefract Castle has played more than its fair share in some of the murkier episodes in England's history. It was here in 1322 that Thomas, Earl of Lancaster was executed, and the deposed King Richard II was either murdered or starved to death in its dungeon. Following the Battle of Wakefield, a number of Yorkist nobles, including Sir Thomas Vaughan, Sir Richard Grey, and the Earl Rivers, were summarily put to death on the orders of Richard III. No wonder Shakespeare referred to the castle as 'bloody Pomfret'.

PENRITH, LOWTHER CASTLE 1894 33512
This is not so much a castle, more a country house,
built for the first Earl of Lonsdale by Sir Robert
Smirke in 1806-11. The previous residence on the site
dated from the 17th century, but had been badly damaged by fire in 1720. Lowther itself
was gutted in 1957.

PENRITH CASTLE 1893 32938
Penrith was one of a number of northern castles built during
the last decades of the 14th century; others included Bolton,
Wressel, Raby and Lumley. The licence to crenellate was granted in 1397 - the castle was considered necessary as a defence
against Scottish raids. Though the castle was enlarged by
Richard, Duke of Gloucester, its career as a fortress was short. A
16th-century survey lists the gatehouse and gates as being in
ruins, and two towers and domestic quarters as being in good
repair. In 1648 Penrith was captured by the Parliamentarians,
who then used it as a quarry, partially demolishing the place
and selling off the stone.

KENDAL CASTLE 1896 38538

The land on which Kendal Castle stands was acquired through marriage by Ivo de Taillebois, and it is he who is thought to have built the original 11th-century fortress. It was also the birthplace of Catherine Parr (1512-1548), sixth and surviving wife of Henry VIII. Kendal appears to have become derelict by the beginning of the 17th century.

KENDAL, SIZERGH CASTLE 1896 38542

The home of the Strickland family for 750 years, Sizergh was originally a 14th-century pele tower with 15th, 16th, and 18th-century additions and alterations, including a Tudor great hall. The superb quality of Sizergh's Tudor woodwork and panelling served as the model for the restoration of Hever Castle by William Waldorf Astor.

COCKERMOUTH CASTLE 1906 54999
Built in the mid-13th century by William de Fortibus,
Cockermouth's defences were enhanced on three sides by its
location at the junction of two rivers. A barbican provided additional defences to the outer gatehouse on the east side, and the
inner and outer wards were divided by a ditch, wall, and inner
gatehouse equipped with a drawbridge. Some of the structure
dates back to William's days, but most is mid to late 14th-centu-
ry, with 18th- and 19th-century buildings
in the outer ward.

PIEL CASTLE 1893 32993
The extensive remains of Piel Castle date from the early 14th century, and are located on Piel Island to the south of Barrow in Furness.

GREYSTOKE CASTLE 1893 32956
The original pele tower erected by William, Lord Greystoke in 1353 can be seen here at the rear of the building. During the 17th and 18th centuries the castle was extended, and in 1839 Anthony Salvin designed and supervised the erection of a mock-Elizabethan front. Salvin returned to Greystoke in 1868 to carry out restoration work following a fire.

BRAMPTON
Naworth Castle c1955 B520006
A minor 14th-century castle, Naworth stands on a triangular
piece of land by the river Irthling with deep ditch defences on
three sides and a moat and drawbridge on the fourth. During
the Civil War Naworth was held for the king. The north-east
tower is known as Belted Will's Tower, named after Lord
William, who as Warden of the Marches took great delight in
hanging wrongdoers from trees in view of the castle. On 10 May
1844 a serious fire destroyed much of the castle; it was later
restored by Anthony Salvin.

CLITHEROE CASTLE 1927 80535

The death of Henry I in 1135 saw England torn apart by civil war. The succession had been settled by Henry on his daughter Matilda, but the throne was seized by Stephen, a grandson of William the Conqueror. As well as being harassed by Matilda's supporters, the North was sorely troubled by Scots raiding parties. In 1137 the English inhabitants and the Norman garrison of Clitheroe Castle joined forces to fight off one such raid. In 1649 Clitheroe was reduced on Cromwell's orders so that it would be of little, if any, strategic importance. In 1660 it was given along with the Honour of Clitheroe by Charles II to General George Monck. Monck had fought for Parliament, but had later been one of the prime movers in bringing about the Restoration.

LANCASTER CASTLE GATEWAY 1896 37369
The first castle at Lancaster was built by Roger de Poitou, though the massive stone keep was added about 1170. King John lavished money on Lancaster, building curtain walls, round towers and Hadrian's Tower. In 1322 Robert the Bruce sacked the town, but was unable to take the castle. Featured here is the gatehouse and flanking octagonal towers built by John of Gaunt, which stand over 60 ft high. It was built of stone salvaged from earlier structures, and equipped with a portcullis and machicolations.

HALTON CASTLE 1900 45439
Built on a rocky outcrop overlooking the Mersey, Halton passed by marriage in 1311 to the House of Lancaster, and was later a favourite hunting lodge of John of Gaunt. When John's son was crowned Henry V, Halton was a part of his Lancastrian inheritance and therefore not Crown property. The castle was remodelled between 1450-57 when a twin-towered gatehouse was added. In 1644 it fell into Parliamentarian hands and was demolished.

LEASOWE CASTLE c1965 L233010
Leasowe was built by Ferdinando, fifth Earl of Derby and Lord of Man in 1593 as a summer residence. During the English Civil War James Stanley, the seventh earl, held the Isle of Man for the King, and Leasowe suffered and fell into ruin. It was known to the locals as Mockbeggar Hall. The castle was rebuilt and the castellated front was added in 1818. Leasowe later became a convalescent home.

BEESTON CASTLE 1888 20655
Built high on a sandstone crag commanding Tarporley Gap,
Beeston was one of a series of fortresses built by Rannulf de
Blundeville, sixth Earl of Chester and Lincoln; the others were
Chartley in Staffordshire and Bolingbroke in Lincolnshire.
Rannulf died before Beeston was finished, with the result that
the domestic buildings were never erected. In 1241 Henry used
the castle to house Welsh prisoners, and in 1303 it was upgraded as part of a series of second-line defences against Welsh
attacks. During the English Civil War it withstood a
year-long siege, surrendering on 16 November 1645. Beeston
also has the deepest well - 366 feet - of any fortress in England.

CHOLMONDELEY CASTLE 1898 42482
Originally built in the late 16th century,
Cholmondeley was heavily remodelled by Vanbrugh;
however, most of his work was subsequently demolished to make way for the present castle, which was
built between 1801 and 1830. It is the seat of the
Marquess of Cholmondeley.

BOLSOVER CASTLE 1902 48905
Here we see the ruins of the once luxurious state rooms of Bolsover Castle. It was probably in these rooms that the Duke of Newcastle lavished thousands of pounds on entertaining Charles I. One such three-day visit by the king in 1634 is said to have set the duke back £15,000, a phenomenal amount of money in 17th-century England.

NOTTINGHAM CASTLE 1890 22845

The Calendars of State Papers Domestic for 9 May 1651 record the proposal for the demolition of Nottingham Castle and the despatch of a troop of dragoons to undertake the task. On 9 June 1651 the report was approved, and demolition of the castle, all outworks and fortifications was ordered to be commenced within fourteen days and completed not later than 10 November 1651. The buildings we see here were built by the Duke of Newcastle as a private residence in 1679, but were burnt out during the Reform Bill Riots of 1831.

NOTTINGHAM CASTLE GATEWAY 1902 48330

There is another unofficial entrance into the castle, known these days as Mortimer's Hole. It was by this secret passage on the south-east side that Edward III is said to have gained entry to the castle to arrest Roger Mortimer, his mother's lover.

TATTERSHALL CASTLE 1893 32081
Tattershall was extensively rebuilt by Ralph Cromwell, a veteran of Agincourt, and Lord Chancellor of England.
Built entirely of brick, an early use of the material on such a large scale, with windows and dressings of Ancaster
limestone, little survives of Tattershall save for its magnificent five-storeyed tower keep. On the top of the keep is
a double fighting platform; Ralph had copied the very latest French practice by building machicolated parapets.
Tattershall was rescued from becoming derelict by Lord Curzon, who refurbished it between 1911 and 1914.

NEWARK CASTLE 1895 35551

It was Alexander, Bishop of Lincoln and lord of the manor, who replaced the original Norman timber fortress with one of stone, employing Ranulph of Durham to build the gatehouse; Newark thus became one of the finest castles in 12th-century England. On 19 October 1216, King John died at Newark Castle, having been poisoned several days earlier by the Cistercian monk, Simon of Swineshead. His body was embalmed and taken to Worcester, where it was buried. Following its surrender to the Parliamentarians at the end of the English Civil War, the castle was ordered to be slighted so that it would be of no further military value. Slighting, however, was carried out to varying degrees: Nottingham Castle was all but destroyed, but at Newark the three-storey gatehouse, three towers and the curtain survived. This photograph shows the north-west wall of the ruined castle towering above the river Trent.

BELVOIR CASTLE c1960 B633078
The first castle on this site was built by Robert de Todeni in the
11th century, and it was improved upon by subsequent owners
until the 1470s, when Lord Hastings ordered it to be dismantled
to provide stone for his castle at Ashby de la Zouche. Belvoir was
rebuilt by the first Earl of Rutland. During the English Civil War
it was twice held by the Royalists, and was besieged by the
unpleasant characters Colonel-General Poyntz and Colonel
Rossiter, who were responsible for allowing the massacre of 140
defenders of Shelford House. Ordered to be slighted, Belvoir
was again rebuilt, but the bulk of the present castle dates from
its rebuilding following a fire in 1816.

KIRBY MUXLOE CASTLE c1965 K126004

Begun by William Lord Hastings in 1480, and never finished, Kirby Muxloe is an early example of the use of brick in castle building. Though equipped with loops for handguns (they are the openings that look like inverted keyholes), Kirby was intended to be more a country house than a fortress. The surviving west tower is where Jane Shore, mistress of Edward IV, came after his death.

ROCKINGHAM CASTLE c1955 R353009

In 1095, Rockingham was the scene of one of the earliest recorded Councils of England, which was held in the Great Hall. Though a royal fortress, Edward I was the last monarch to undertake large scale repairs and reconstruction; by the beginning of the 16th century it was in a dilapidated condition. In 1530 Edward Watson leased Rockingham from Henry VIII and set about restoring it.

CAVERSWALL CASTLE c1955 C691001

Situated one and a half miles north of Blythe Bridge railway station in Staffordshire, Caverswall's history certainly goes back to at least 1275 when Walter de Caverswell was granted a licence to crenellate. The castle was rebuilt in the 1640s by Matthew Cradock, first governor of Massachusetts. It is in the Jacobean style, with a tower imitating the medieval period.

TUTBURY CASTLE c1955 T165006

Built on a natural defensive site that had been used since the Bronze Age, Tutbury was garrisoned by Royalist troops during the Civil War. On 6 July 1644, Sir John Gell led his Parliamentarian force on a lightning raid, but was unable to take the fortress. Tutbury held out until April 1646, when it was forced to surrender due to an outbreak of the plague.

ALTON CASTLE c1955 A285001

Perched high on its hill, Alton Castle dominates the area. The original castle is thought to have been built by Bertram de Verdun, who also founded the Cistercian abbey at Croxden. In 1407 it passed by marriage to John Talbot, after being in the possession of the Furnivalle family for about one hundred years. It was rebuilt during the 15th century, badly damaged during the English Civil War, and rebuilt again. The castle was never a main residence for the Talbot family, though the sixteenth earl commissioned Pugin to rebuild the place. The remains of the old castle are in the grounds.

TAMWORTH CASTLE c1955 T157022

The Normans built a wooden motte and bailey castle at Tamworth soon after the conquest on the site of the Mercian fortifications of 913, but this was replaced by the shell-keep and tower that still stand. By the mid-16th century much of the castle is said to have been in ruins, though some construction work was done at this time, including the superb banqueting hall. The castle was sold to the corporation in 1897 by the 5th Marquess of Townsend. The gatehouse seen here dates from the 13th century.

ECCLESHALL CASTLE c1965 E18023

In 1209 the rebuilding of Eccleshall Castle was begun by Walter Langton, Bishop of Lichfield and Lord High Treasurer of England. During the Civil War it was garrisoned by Royalist troops, but it fell in August 1643 after a siege lasting eight weeks. In 1695 Bishop Lloyd began rebuilding the castle, and it continued as a residence until the death of Bishop Lonsdale in 1867.

STAFFORD CASTLE C1955 S411002
The first castle on this site is thought to have been built by Robert de Stafford during the 1070s. The timber keep was replaced by one built of stone, and about 1350 the fortress underwent extensive rebuilding. During the Civil War the castle was ably defended by the Dowager Lady Stafford, but after it had fallen it was ordered to be slighted. In the early 19th century rebuilding began, but the project was abandoned before completion.

WARWICK CASTLE 1892 30998

Henry de Newburgh built a large wooden motte and bailey on the site of the present castle; before his death in 1123 he might well have begun to replace the wood with stone. During the Barons' War, Warwick was sacked and all but destroyed by forces loyal to Simon de Montfort. In 1268 the earldom passed to the Beauchamp family, who set about the task of rebuilding. This photograph shows the domestic range, which is situated on the southern side of the fortress overlooking the river. The roof of the Great Hall and several other rooms were restored at considerable cost after being seriously damaged by fire in 1871.

KENILWORTH CASTLE 1922 72405

The first castle to be built at Kenilworth is thought to have been a motte and bailey constructed between 1122 and 1127 by Geoffrey de Clinton. It was de Clinton's son who built the keep. One of Kenilworth's prisoners was the deposed Edward II, who was held here prior to his transfer to Berkeley Castle where he was murdered with a red-hot poker. It was John of Gaunt who set about transforming Kenilworth from a Norman fortress to a Gothic palace. Work began around 1389, with only the keep being retained. The entire inner ward was rebuilt; it included a great hall, private apartments, kitchens and store rooms. On the left is Leicester's gatehouse, which had been converted into a private dwelling.

LUDLOW CASTLE 1910 62479

Perched on its cliff overlooking the rivers Teme and Corve, Ludlow was built in a strategic location on the Welsh borders. The castle was probably begun by Roger de Lacy in 1080, and it was Sir John de Dinan who built the chapel with its unusual circular nave in 1130. By 1311, Ludlow was in the hands of Roger de Mortimer, first Earl of March, and later the lover of Queen Isabella and murderer of Edward II. Mortimer became a threat to the young Edward III, and in 1330 he was seized at Nottingham and hanged.

BERKELEY CASTLE c1955 B72033

Roger de Berkeley, the first tenant after the Conquest, was probably responsible for the construction of the first castle on the site, and we know that Henry II was entertained here over Easter in 1121. The erection of the stone shell keep began about 1156; it underwent extensive remodelling during the 14th century, when Thomas, third Lord Berkeley, had two of the semi-circular bastions replaced and two others incorporated into the structure of the keep.

BROUGHTON CASTLE 1922 72110
The castle was originally a fortified manor house built by Sir
John de Broughton in 1306; the battlements and a gatehouse
were added by William de Wykeham in 1405. Broughton passed
by marriage to the Fiennes family, who were responsible for the
fine Tudor building we see here.

BERKHAMSTED CASTLE c1955 B407050
It was once one of the most important castles in the country,
but little now survives of Berkhamsted except for the motte.
Here are the remains of a circular keep, the southern barbican,
and two wing walls on the south side of the motte. The original
castle was owned by Robert of Mortain, the Conqueror's half-
brother, though perhaps its most famous resident was Thomas
Becket, who lived here for ten years when he was Chancellor.
The castle was besieged by Prince Louis of France in 1216, and
some earthworks beyond the outer ditch are claimed by some to
be where Louis positioned his catapults. Much of the outer
works were destroyed during the 1830s with the
building of the railway.

FARNHAM CASTLE 1935 86755

Farnham had been an ecclesiastical estate since the 7th century, but it was Henry of Blois, Bishop of Winchester from 1129-1171, who began building a castle when he ordered the raising of a motte and tower in 1138. This structure does not appear to have lasted too long; it is believed that it was demolished on the orders of Henry II in 1155. The ruins date from the late 12th to the late 15th century; two principal builders were William of Wykenham, who was Bishop from 1367-1404, and Bishop Waynflete, who was responsible for the building of the brick tower between 1470 and 1475.

GUILDFORD CASTLE 1933 85753

Little remains of Guildford Castle, once a favourite royal residence where many princes of the blood were brought up. The original Norman castle was built partially on an earlier Anglo-Saxon fortification, a stone keep being added in the 12th century. Apart from the remains of the keep shown here, an arch from the outer gateway still stands in Quarry Street.

BUNGAY CASTLE c1965 B617053

The ruins of Bungay date from the reign of Edward I, but there was once an earlier castle on the site which had been owned by Hugh Bigod, Earl of Norfolk. When Henry II came to the throne, he resolved the lack of royal castles in Suffolk by confiscating four of Hugh's. Although Bungay and Framlington were later restored to him, Hugh made the mistake of joining a rebellion against the King; Bungay and Framlington were confiscated for a second time, and ordered to be dismantled.

TONBRIDGE CASTLE c1950 T101078

Situated on the north bank of the Medway, the original motte and bailey castle was replaced with stone by the early 13th century, when the shell keep was built. Here we see the keep-gatehouse, which is thought to have been built around 1300; the view shows the two small towers at the rear of the structure. Gatehouse defences included a draw-bridge and two main portcullises; there were others protecting doorways off the entrance passageway, and a number of murder holes were also incorporated into the design.

CHILHAM CASTLE 1903 50346
The castle is situated five miles west of Canterbury; all that remains of the Norman fortress is a part of the keep in the north-west angle. The present castle is a Jacobean mansion built by Sir Dudley Digges in 1616, and is the seat of Viscount Massereene and Ferrard.

ROCHESTER CASTLE 1908 59883

This was one of the earliest castles in England to be constructed from stone (in about 1090); the massive 125ft-high keep, the tallest in the country, was added by William de Corbeil, Archbishop of Canterbury, in 1127. Rochester was besieged by King John in 1215 after Archbishop Langton had refused to surrender the fortress to the bishop of Winchester. With the siege failing to make any headway, John resorted to mining, and ordered 'forty of the fattest pigs of the sort least good for eating to bring fire beneath the tower'. Though a whole section of the tower collapsed, the siege was not over: the defenders simply withdrew behind a great cross-wall, and it was only starvation that eventually forced them out.

HEVER CASTLE 1891 29396

Built in the 13th century, and later the home of Anne Boleyn, Hever was rescued from obscurity by William Waldorf Astor, who bought it in 1903 and spent a fortune restoring it to its former glory. When this picture was taken, Hever was in good condition, but had been reduced to nothing more than a farmhouse.

LEEDS CASTLE c1955 M9079

Built on the site of a 9th-century royal manor house, Leeds Castle became a royal fortress on the accession of Edward I. It served as a royal residence for six medieval queens, and it was a favourite haunt of Henry VIII, Queen Eleanor of Castile and Catherine of Valois. The Leeds Castle Foundation was established in 1974 to preserve the place as a 'living' castle through income generated from visitors, conferencing and special events.

SALTWOOD CASTLE 1890 25896
It was from here that four knights set off one winter evening in
1170 for Canterbury to murder Thomas Becket. It was King
John who granted Saltwood to the Archbishops of Canterbury,
but it was returned to the Crown by Archbishop Cranmer. In
more recent times it was the home of the historian and MP for
Kensington and Chelsea, Alan Clark (1928-1999), an eccentric,
clever, outrageous, eloquent, irreverent and amusing man
whose diaries became a best-seller. His book 'The Donkeys'
(1961) was a savage assault on British military ineptness during
the Great War. It was turned into the hit left-wing musical 'Oh
What A Lovely War'.

ALLINGTON CASTLE 1898 41547

The wooden fortifications at Allington were soon replaced with stone; it is thought that the work was carried out by Gundulf, the Conqueror's master builder, who was also responsible for the Tower of London. It was at Allington that the plotters against the marriage between Queen Mary and Philip of Spain first met. Their rebellion ended in disaster, and Sir Thomas Wyatt of Allington went to the block.

DOVER CASTLE 1890 25705

Henry II's great keep stands high above the mural towers of the inner bailey. It was under Henry and his son Richard I that Dover was transformed into one of the greatest fortresses in the kingdom. The inner bailey was defended by fourteen towers, and both gates had barbicans. The castle was besieged by Prince Louis of France in 1216, but it held out, even though the north gate was successfully mined. The threat of invasion from France, and later from Spain, meant that Dover's defences were kept in a good state of repair and upgraded when necessary.

BRAMBER CASTLE c1955

Destroyed during the English Civil War, Bramber is thought to have originally been built in the 11th century by William de Braose. The site is on the banks of the river Adur about a mile from Steyning on the present A283; it made use of both a natural mound and a pre-Conquest earthwork. All that remains are fragments of the tower keep and the curtain wall.

AMBERLEY CASTLE GATEHOUSE 1898

Those of you familiar with Amberley will see that this picture pre-dates the restoration of the battlements on the 14th-century gatehouse. The castle was originally a manor house belonging to the Bishops of Chichester; a licence to crenellate was granted in 1377. The castle was dismantled by the Parliamentarians during the English Civil War.

BRAMBER CASTLE c1955 B179009

AMBERLEY CASTLE GATEHOUSE 1898 42553

ARUNDEL CASTLE 1906 56725

Roger de Montgomery was a man William the Conqueror could trust. De Montgomery was awarded Arundel, and given responsibility for defending the Sussex coast against possible French raids or even an invasion, both of which were considered a real threat. The original castle, raised around 1068, comprised a 70ft high motte and two baileys, built on the site of an Anglo-Saxon fortification. Robert de Belesme is thought to have begun building the circular stone shell keep; the work continued under Henry I and Henry II after Arundel had become a royal fortress. Badly damaged during the English Civil War, Arundel has undergone a considerable amount of rebuilding. It was transformed into a Gothic pile during the Napoleonic period, and rebuilt yet again between 1890 and 1903.

BODIAM CASTLE 1890 25390

Bodiam is a 14th-century moated castle, restored, like Tattershall in Lincolnshire, by Lord Curzon. The original approach was along a wooden bridge at right angles to the castle walls, thus exposing an attacker's unshielded flank to fire from the defenders. Details are difficult to make out in this pre-restoration photograph, but in front of the gateway tower is the ruined barbican, and in front of that is the much overgrown octagonal island, which at one time might also have been fortified. Bodiam was protected by three drawbridges, two fortified bastions, three portcullises, and an internal arrangement of rooms and doorways designed for defence.

RYE, YPRES CASTLE 1912 64929

Despite carrying the title of Ypres Castle in 1912, this structure was called the Badding Tower when it was built in the 13th century, and was a place of refuge during French raids on the town. In 1377 the French burnt Rye to the ground, but the tower survived. It was eventually sold to a John de Ypres, though it later served as a prison. The detached battlemented tower was added during the 19th century.

HASTINGS CASTLE 1925 77965

The ruins of Hastings Castle are believed to stand on the site where William the Conqueror built his first castle in England; this was a wooden prefabricated structure shipped over with his invasion force. The present ruins date from the 11th and 12th centuries.

NORWICH CASTLE 1891 28177
The Tombland Fair provides the activity in this picture
of Norwich Castle. At the time of the Conquest,
Norwich was both an important town and a major
port. Control was quickly established with the erection
of one of the earliest motte and bailey castles in
England. A stone keep was built by Henry I, but the
one seen here is the result of much rebuilding,
both inside and out.

COLCHESTER CASTLE 1892 31524

Construction of Colchester Castle is thought to have started
around 1080, and in 1101 it was granted to Eudo the Steward by
Henry I. The builders used salvaged Roman stone, and the keep
was raised to at least three storeys. In 1215 it was occupied by
French troops and besieged by King John in person; the French
withdrew on the accession of Henry III. The castle was eventually bought by John Wheeley for its raw materials, but he had only
demolished the top of the keep before the castle was saved by
the lawyer and antiquarian Charles Grey.

It became a museum in 1931.

CASTLE RISING 1898 40894

Built by William de Albini in the 12th century, Castle Rising sits inside a ringwork, with a small bailey on either side; these defences may originally have been constructed of wood. The keep is built from local stone, and contains a Great Hall, chapel, kitchen, a chamber, and a combined buttery and pantry. There are also two latrines, one of which contains a urinal: were they designed for use by different sexes?

HADLEIGH CASTLE c1955 H167007

Construction of Hadleigh began in the 13th century, when Baron Hubert de Burgh was granted a licence to build. Seized by Henry III in an unfinished state, Hadleigh was completed as a counter to French raids along the Essex coast. This photograph shows the ruins of the two towers at the east end of the curtain wall, the remains of which still stand three storeys high. Hadleigh was a favourite residence of Edward III.

WINDSOR CASTLE 1914 66985
Windsor is thought to have been founded by William
the Conqueror. It consisted of a large motte, on top of
which was built a timber tower protected by palisades;
the motte divided the Upper and Lower Wards.
However, though Windsor is thought to date from
around 1070, the earliest written record is the entry in
the Domesday survey of 1086.

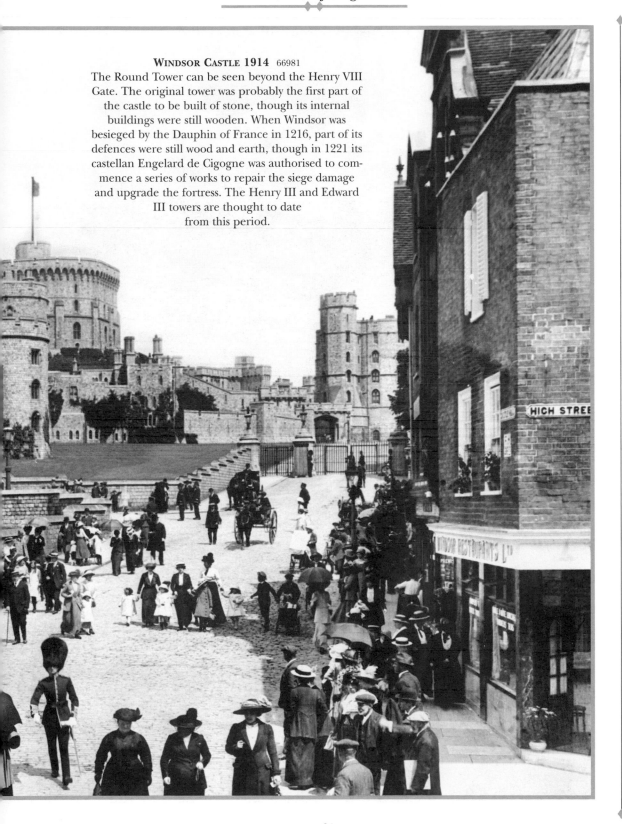

WINDSOR CASTLE 1914 66981
The Round Tower can be seen beyond the Henry VIII
Gate. The original tower was probably the first part of
the castle to be built of stone, though its internal
buildings were still wooden. When Windsor was
besieged by the Dauphin of France in 1216, part of its
defences were still wood and earth, though in 1221 its
castellan Engelard de Cigogne was authorised to com-
mence a series of works to repair the siege damage
and upgrade the fortress. The Henry III and Edward
III towers are thought to date
from this period.

WINDSOR CASTLE, THE EAST TERRACE 1895 35362

DONNINGTON CASTLE c1955 N61008

WINDSOR CASTLE
The East Terrace 1895
The East Terrace dates from Wyatville's remodelling of 1843. From left to right we have the Kings (now Victoria) Tower; the Clarence Tower; the Chester Tower, which houses the library; and the Prince of Wales Tower. In 1800 the King's Tower was known as the South East Tower, and the Prince of Wales Tower was called the Board of Green Cloth Tower.

◆

DONNINGTON CASTLE c1955
Set high on a spur of land overlooking the river Lambourne, Donnington was probably founded in the 11th century; it eventually became the property of Sir Richard de Abberbury. In 1386, Sir Richard was granted a licence to crenellate, and he built the gatehouse flanked by two circular towers which are 65ft high. During the Civil War it was besieged twice.

OLD SARUM, THE CASTLE RUINS C1965 O58013
Old Sarum was one of a number of ancient sites refortified by
the Normans; others included Thetford (Norfolk), Rochester
(Kent) and Carisbrooke (Isle of Wight). The site, which included the town, is on a steep-sided mound, thought to be an Iron
Age hill fort. Around 1078 the Episcopal See of Sherborne was
transferred to Old Sarum, and a Norman cathedral and a bishop's castle were built; the motte was in the centre of the town-
ship. Following King Stephen's annexation of the bishop's castles in 1139, relations between the clergy and the military wors-
ened. In 1220 a new cathedral was founded at New Sarum
(Salisbury), and the old church was abandoned and later
demolished. Although the castle was garrisoned during the
reign of Edward II, it had been abandoned by the middle
of the 15th century.

DEVIZES CASTLE 1898 42308
There was certainly a castle here of sorts in 1106, as Robert Curthose, elder son of the Conqueror, was held prisoner here after being defeated at Tinchebrai. It was Robert's brother Henry I who built the first castle of any consequence at Devizes, and this was enlarged by Bishop Roger. By the 17th century little remained, the castle having been used as a quarry by local people. The present structure dates mainly from 1842.

LUDGERSHALL CASTLE c1965 L109006
This was a favourite hunting lodge of Henry III. Royal requirements were that a number of additional domestic buildings were erected, including apartments for the queen, the king's son and heir, and members of the household. King John ordered new kitchens to be built both here and at Marlborough. 'In each kitchen shall be made a hearth for the cooking of two or three oxen'.

LONGFORD CASTLE 1887 19820

This photograph shows Longford a few years after Anthony Salvin had rebuilt the facade. The original was built by Sir Thomas Gorges on his 250 acre estate at Bodenham. He ran out of money at one stage, and it was only owing to his being granted salvage from an Armada wreck that he had funds to finish the project. Gorges' castle celebrated the Holy Trinity in its construction: it was triangular in shape, with a round tower on each of the three corners. Bodenham was extensively altered during the 19th century.

CORFE CASTLE 1897 40318

William the Conqueror's original royal fortress was a wooden tower on the motte, which in later generations would form the upper bailey. Quite early on, the motte's defences were improved with the building of a stone wall around it, and the earliest stone building appears to have been a hall in the western bailey. In this photograph we see the remains of Henry I's great stone tower keep, and to its right is the western bailey where King John built new private apartments. In the foreground is the southern bailey walled by Henry III, and the drum-towered gatehouse built by Edward I. The castle was slighted in 1646 on the orders of Parliament, and the keep and walls blown up with gunpowder.

CHRISTCHURCH CASTLE 1900 45050

This was a former royal manor granted by Henry I to his cousin Richard de Redvers in 1100, who raised the first castle on the site, building a motte 27ft high. The hall, seen here, dates from 1160-80. Its east side fronts the river, and thus forms a part of the curtain wall; as we can see, the lower windows are looped for defence. Even though Christchurch saw little action during the English Civil War, the castle was ordered to be demolished. In May 1650 further slighting was ordered, and in the following November the Governor of Southampton was ordered to oversee the work.

PORCHESTER CASTLE 1898 42708

The original Norman fort at Porchester was merely a corner of the old 3rd-century Roman Saxon Shore fort defended on the two open sides by the building of a wooden palisade. It was after the rebellion against Henry I by his elder brother Robert Curthose that the decision was taken to build a castle proper. The tower keep, which when built was only one storey high, has walls twelve feet thick, and when two further floors were added it was similar to those at Falaise, Norwich and Corfe. Excavations in the areas of the great hall and lodgings have revealed bones of animals and birds used for food. The finds did not include bones from parts of the body which were not edible, which leads archaeologists to believe that food preparation took place elsewhere.

CARISBROOKE CASTLE c1955 C26035

The castle is famous for its associations with Charles I: he was held here from November 1647 to the autumn of 1648, prior to his transfer to the mainland and his trial and subsequent execution. The earthworks are mainly 11th- and 12th-century, and none of the domestic buildings of the Norman fortress survives. The most impressive feature is the gatehouse, which dates from the 14th century with later additions. In 1377 the French landed on the Isle of Wight; they failed to take the castle, which was defended by Sir Hugh Tyrell. Following the threat from Spain in 1588, the Italian fortifications engineer Federigo Gianibelli was commissioned to improve Carisbrooke's defences; his curtain walls and bastions are still in very good condition.

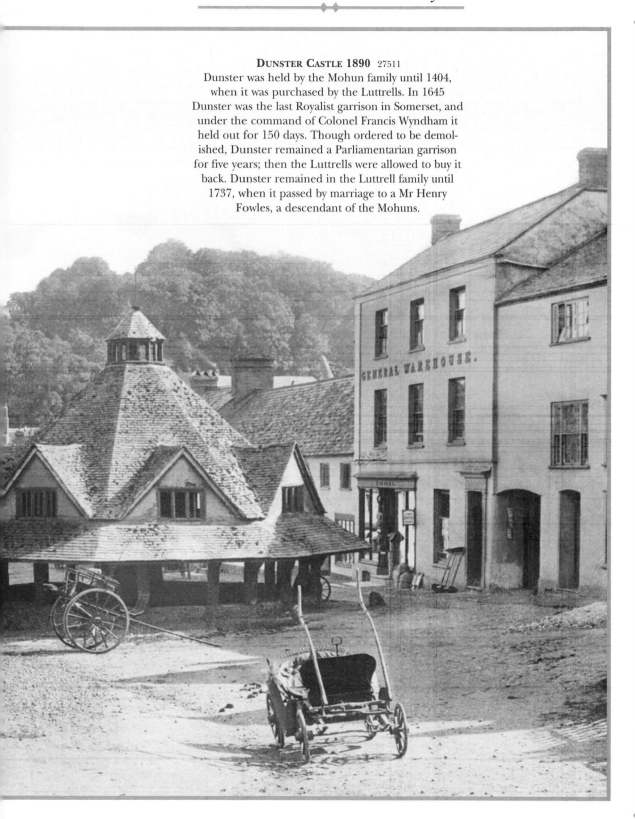

DUNSTER CASTLE 1890 27511

Dunster was held by the Mohun family until 1404, when it was purchased by the Luttrells. In 1645 Dunster was the last Royalist garrison in Somerset, and under the command of Colonel Francis Wyndham it held out for 150 days. Though ordered to be demolished, Dunster remained a Parliamentarian garrison for five years; then the Luttrells were allowed to buy it back. Dunster remained in the Luttrell family until 1737, when it passed by marriage to a Mr Henry Fowles, a descendant of the Mohuns.

HENBURY, BLAISE CASTLE c1955 H164303
This is not so much a castle, more a gentleman's folly. Blaise,
with its four castellated towers, was built in 1771 by Thomas
Farr. In 1765 Thomas had been a member of a delegation sent
by the Society of Merchant Venturers, of which he later became
Master, to deliver a petition to Parliament against the renewal of
the Sugar Act. The government intended to use the provisions
of the Act to make the American colonies pay for their own
defence and to contribute towards the costs of the Seven Years
War. The merchants had close links with the colonists, and
knew more of American opinion than the entire government
put together. They realised that the Act would harm relations
with the colonists and damage trade - and they were right.

WALTON CASTLE 1913 65422

The castle stands to the north-east of Clevedon. It is not in fact a castle, but an early example of a folly, and it was probably built as a ruin to start with. It now stands in the middle of a golf course, and is probably highly dangerous to go exploring in.

FARLEIGH HUNGERFORD CASTLE 1907 57756

This was originally a manor house. The fortification of Farleigh Montfort was begun around 1370 by Sir Thomas de Hungerford before he had been granted a licence to crenellate, though he was granted a pardon in 1383. His son, Sir Walter, served as Treasurer of England to Henry V, and he extended the castle in the 1420s, adding among other things the east gate, seen here covered with ivy. The gate originally had a drawbridge. In 1426 Sir Walter was created Lord Hungerford, and the castle's name was changed to Farleigh Hungerford.

FARLEIGH HUNGERFORD CASTLE 1900 45366

The castle was briefly owned by Richard, Duke of Gloucester, who later presented it to the Duke of Norfolk. By one of those twists of fate the Duke, along with Richard, was killed at Bosworth in August 1485. The following year Sir Walter Hungerford regained the castle for his family, the twist being that Sir Walter had been knighted on the field of Bosworth.

RESTORMEL CASTLE 1891 29851

This photograph shows the ivy-smothered shell keep and gatehouse of Restormel Castle at a time when the ruin was still a titular possession of the Prince of Wales. The projecting gatehouse was added about 1100, and the work of replacing the timber palisading with stone occurred sometime during the second half of the 13th century. Edmund, Earl of Cornwall completed the modernisation of Restormel by replacing the internal wooden buildings with stone.

LAUNCESTON CASTLE 1909

Launceston was probably built shortly after the suppression of a Cornish rebellion in 1068. The motte was surrounded by a ditch, but this came within the castle perimeter when the gate tower was built, so a second ditch was excavated. The main buildings on the motte were approached by a staircase, and the keep was defended by a portcullis.

◆

ST MICHAEL'S MOUNT 1908

The original building on the mount was a priory founded by Edward the Confessor in 1044. When Richard I was away fighting in the Third Crusade, the Mount was seized for John by Henry de Pomeroy, though it was subsequently retaken by Richard, who stationed a permanent garrison here. The monks were finally expelled in 1425, and St Michael's became a fortress. It was involved in several rebellions against the Crown; the last was the Cornish uprising against Edward IV.

LAUNCESTON CASTLE 1909 61309

ST MICHAEL'S MOUNT 1908 60984

TINTAGEL CASTLE 1894 33595A
Perched on rocky cliffs five miles north-west of Camelford, Tintagel probably owes its survival to its association with the Arthurian legends. The castle itself dates from c1145, and was built by Reginald, Earl of Cornwall, a bastard son of Henry I. The ruins date from the 12th to the 15th centuries, and it was opened to the public in 1852.

SALTASH, TREMATON CASTLE c1965 S50144

SALTASH
Trematon Castle c1965

Trematon was a 12th-century motte and bailey castle. It was extensively rebuilt in the 13th century with a shell keep, bailey wall, and a strong gatehouse on the south-west side. The shell keep is about 70ft long by 50ft wide, and its 10ft-thick walls still stand to a height of 30ft.

◆

BUDE CASTLE 1893

Situated to the west of Stratton, Bude Castle was built on a promontory by Sir Goldsworthy Gurney in 1850. Gurney was an inventor: one of his innovations was the introduction of steam-powered stagecoaches on the London to Bath route. Gurney did not have long to enjoy Bude, for he died in 1853.

BUDE CASTLE 1893 31888

COMPTON CASTLE 1890 25936

Compton Castle, near Marlton in Devonshire, is a 14th-century manor house built without a moat, though the gate-house came complete with machicolations. Extensive alterations were carried out when Sir Humphrey Gilbert lived here, and in 1808 the estate was sold off in job lots. The castle was bought by a John Bishop, who demolished some buildings and converted what was left into a farmhouse.

OKEHAMPTON CASTLE 1890 22589

The original castle was built on this site by Baldwin FitzGerald
following his appointment by William the Conqueror as Sheriff
of Devonshire. It was from here that FitzGerald ruthlessly put
down a rebellion in the south-west. The castle was rebuilt in the
14th century when an extension was added to the keep, and
Okehampton became more a residence than a fortress. Though
defended during the English Civil War, the castle had in fact
been partially dismantled around 1538 following the execution
of its owner, the Marquess of Exeter, for his alleged role in a
plot against Henry VIII. During a confused skirmish at dawn on
8 February 1643, the poet Sidney Godolphin was killed.

PENDENNIS CASTLE 1890 24227

The central tower was built in 1540-45, and was designed so that guns could be mounted on the roof as well as on the two gun decks inside. The wall to the right is a part of the second-phase lower battery which gave Pendennis a further fourteen gun positions. The northern entrance block ,which included the governor's lodging, marks the third building phase; it was completed in c1550.

ST MAWES CASTLE 1938 88813

St Mawes comprises a central tower and three smaller lobes, so that from the air it resembles a clover leaf. The circular keep is taller than that at Pendennis, and contains four floors; the approach from the landward side is by way of a drawbridge. St Mawes is sited on lower ground 'the better to annoy shipping'.

FOWEY, ST CATHERINE'S CASTLE c1955 F43115

Once one of the most important ports west of Bristol, Fowey in 1346 was wealthy enough to contribute 47 ships and over 700 men to Edward III's blockade of Calais. Still a major port in the 1530s, defences consisted of a chain link boom and a shore battery mounted at St Catherine's Castle.

POLRUAN TOWER c1965 P69069

This predates Henry's defences by almost one hundred years. In 1457 the French launched a raid against Fowey Harbour, and as a result a boom defence was added. There were two towers, one at Fowey, and this one at Polruan, and it was between these that the chain was stretched. The towers mounted small calibre guns, and were designed so that the staircase to the battlements was separate from that between the ground and first floor.

HURST CASTLE c1955 M303166

Situated to the south-east of Milford Church, Hurst Castle was probably built between 1539 and 1544 and comprises a twelve-sided central tower protected by a curtain wall and semi-circular bastion towers, and mounting 24 guns. It was here in 1648 that Charles I was held whilst awaiting trial.

NETLEY CASTLE c1955 N10085

Netley, on the east bank of Southampton Water, was another of Henry VIII's coastal forts, though this one was a conversion of an existing building, the gatehouse of Netley Abbey. In 1851 Netley was extensively rebuilt, creating the Gothic pile we see here. It was at this time that the tower was added.

WEYMOUTH, SANDSFOOT CASTLE 1898 41138

Just one mile from Weymouth stand the remains of
Sandsfoot Castle. Originally the fort comprised a two-
storey building with a north tower and a gatehouse.
Another fort to have suffered from erosion is Sandown
Castle on the Isle of Wight, which was built close to
the beach in 1545. Sandown was one of the earliest
forts to be built with an arrow-head bastion, which
enabled the guns to have
wider arcs of fire.

WALMER CASTLE 1892 31435

Along with Deal and Sandown, Walmer was one of the 'Three Castles which keep the Downs'. It was built in 1539-40 with a central circular keep around which were added four semi-circular bastion towers. The gatehouse was equipped with a portcullis and drawbridge, and close defence was provided by murder-holes. Walmer was subsequently modified and converted into the official residence of the Lords Warden of the Cinque Ports - the towns of Hastings, Romney, Hythe, Dover and Sandwich - which were originally responsible for the defence of the Channel. The castellation was added during modifications in 1874.

SANDGATE CASTLE 1903 50371

Situated between Hythe and Folkestone, Sandgate Castle was yet another of Henry VIII's fortifications; it was built with rounded bastions in the German style. The problem with this type of design was that enemy gunners were offered a fairly large target, though it was hoped that cannon balls would bounce off the rounded edges. In 1806 Sandgate was converted into a Martello Tower.

DEAL CASTLE 1894 34217

Built in c1538-40, Deal was equipped with three tiers of platforms for mounting long-range guns for use against shipping, and with handgun embrasures for an all-round defence capability. It is thought that Deal might well have been designed by Henry himself, as the King took more than a passing fancy to the use of artillery.

Index

Frith Book Co Titles

www.francisfrith.co.uk

The Frith Book Company publishes over 100 new titles each year. A selection of those currently available is listed below. For latest catalogue please contact Frith Book Co.

Town Books 96 pages, approximately 100 photos. **County and Themed Books** 128 pages, approximately 150 photos (unless specified). All titles hardback with laminated case and jacket, except those indicated pb (paperback)

Amersham, Chesham & Rickmansworth (pb)	1-85937-340-2	£9.99	Devon (pb)	1-85937-297-x	£9.99
Andover (pb)	1-85937-292-9	£9.99	Devon Churches (pb)	1-85937-250-3	£9.99
Aylesbury (pb)	1-85937-227-9	£9.99	Dorchester (pb)	1-85937-307-0	£9.99
Barnstaple (pb)	1-85937-300-3	£9.99	Dorset (pb)	1-85937-269-4	£9.99
Basildon Living Memories (pb)	1-85937-515-4	£9.99	Dorset Coast (pb)	1-85937-299-6	£9.99
Bath (pb)	1-85937-419-0	£9.99	Dorset Living Memories (pb)	1-85937-584-7	£9.99
Bedford (pb)	1-85937-205-8	£9.99	Down the Severn (pb)	1-85937-560-x	£9.99
Bedfordshire Living Memories	1-85937-513-8	£14.99	Down The Thames (pb)	1-85937-278-3	£9.99
Belfast (pb)	1-85937-303-8	£9.99	Down the Trent	1-85937-311-9	£14.99
Berkshire (pb)	1-85937-191-4	£9.99	East Anglia (pb)	1-85937-265-1	£9.99
Berkshire Churches	1-85937-170-1	£17.99	East Grinstead (pb)	1-85937-138-8	£9.99
Berkshire Living Memories	1-85937-332-1	£14.99	East London	1-85937-080-2	£14.99
Black Country	1-85937-497-2	£12.99	East Sussex (pb)	1-85937-606-1	£9.99
Blackpool (pb)	1-85937-393-3	£9.99	Eastbourne (pb)	1-85937-399-2	£9.99
Bognor Regis (pb)	1-85937-431-x	£9.99	Edinburgh (pb)	1-85937-193-0	£8.99
Bournemouth (pb)	1-85937-545-6	£9.99	England In The 1880s	1-85937-331-3	£17.99
Bradford (pb)	1-85937-204-x	£9.99	Essex - Second Selection	1-85937-456-5	£14.99
Bridgend (pb)	1-85937-386-0	£7.99	Essex (pb)	1-85937-270-8	£9.99
Bridgwater (pb)	1-85937-305-4	£9.99	Essex Coast	1-85937-342-9	£14.99
Bridport (pb)	1-85937-327-5	£9.99	Essex Living Memories	1-85937-490-5	£14.99
Brighton (pb)	1-85937-192-2	£8.99	Exeter	1-85937-539-1	£9.99
Bristol (pb)	1-85937-264-3	£9.99	Exmoor (pb)	1-85937-608-8	£9.99
British Life A Century Ago (pb)	1-85937-213-9	£9.99	Falmouth (pb)	1-85937-594-4	£9.99
Buckinghamshire (pb)	1-85937-200-7	£9.99	Folkestone (pb)	1-85937-124-8	£9.99
Camberley (pb)	1-85937-222-8	£9.99	Frome (pb)	1-85937-317-8	£9.99
Cambridge (pb)	1-85937-422-0	£9.99	Glamorgan	1-85937-488-3	£14.99
Cambridgeshire (pb)	1-85937-420-4	£9.99	Glasgow (pb)	1-85937-190-6	£9.99
Cambridgeshire Villages	1-85937-523-5	£14.99	Glastonbury (pb)	1-85937-338-0	£7.99
Canals And Waterways (pb)	1-85937-291-0	£9.99	Gloucester (pb)	1-85937-232-5	£9.99
Canterbury Cathedral (pb)	1-85937-179-5	£9.99	Gloucestershire (pb)	1-85937-561-8	£9.99
Cardiff (pb)	1-85937-093-4	£9.99	Great Yarmouth (pb)	1-85937-426-3	£9.99
Carmarthenshire (pb)	1-85937-604-5	£9.99	Greater Manchester (pb)	1-85937-266-x	£9.99
Chelmsford (pb)	1-85937-310-0	£9.99	Guildford (pb)	1-85937-410-7	£9.99
Cheltenham (pb)	1-85937-095-0	£9.99	Hampshire (pb)	1-85937-279-1	£9.99
Cheshire (pb)	1-85937-271-6	£9.99	Harrogate (pb)	1-85937-423-9	£9.99
Chester (pb)	1-85937-382 8	£9.99	Hastings and Bexhill (pb)	1-85937-131-0	£9.99
Chesterfield (pb)	1-85937-378-x	£9.99	Heart of Lancashire (pb)	1-85937-197-3	£9.99
Chichester (pb)	1-85937-228-7	£9.99	Helston (pb)	1-85937-214-7	£9.99
Churches of East Cornwall (pb)	1-85937-249-x	£9.99	Hereford (pb)	1-85937-175-2	£9.99
Churches of Hampshire (pb)	1-85937-207-4	£9.99	Herefordshire (pb)	1-85937-567-7	£9.99
Cinque Ports & Two Ancient Towns	1-85937-492-1	£14.99	Herefordshire Living Memories	1-85937-514-6	£14.99
Colchester (pb)	1-85937-188-4	£8.99	Hertfordshire (pb)	1-85937-247-3	£9.99
Cornwall (pb)	1-85937-229-5	£9.99	Horsham (pb)	1-85937-432-8	£9.99
Cornwall Living Memories	1-85937-248-1	£14.99	Humberside (pb)	1-85937-605-3	£9.99
Cotswolds (pb)	1-85937-230-9	£9.99	Hythe, Romney Marsh, Ashford (pb)	1-85937-256-2	£9.99
Cotswolds Living Memories	1-85937-255-4	£14.99	Ipswich (pb)	1-85937-424-7	£9.99
County Durham (pb)	1-85937-398-4	£9.99	Isle of Man (pb)	1-85937-268-6	£9.99
Croydon Living Memories (pb)	1-85937-162-0	£9.99	Isle of Wight (pb)	1-85937-429-8	£9.99
Cumbria (pb)	1-85937-621-5	£9.99	Isle of Wight Living Memories	1-85937-304-6	£14.99
Derby (pb)	1-85937-367-4	£9.99	Kent (pb)	1-85937-189-2	£9.99
Derbyshire (pb)	1-85937-196-5	£9.99	Kent Living Memories(pb)	1-85937-401-8	£9.99
Derbyshire Living Memories	1-85937-330-5	£14.99	Kings Lynn (pb)	1-85937-334-8	£9.99

Available from your local bookshop or from the publisher

Frith Book Co Titles (continued)

Title	ISBN	Price	Title	ISBN	Price
Lake District (pb)	1-85937-275-9	£9.99	Sherborne (pb)	1-85937-301-1	£9.99
Lancashire Living Memories	1-85937-335-6	£14.99	Shrewsbury (pb)	1-85937-325-9	£9.99
Lancaster, Morecambe, Heysham (pb)	1-85937-233-3	£9.99	Shropshire (pb)	1-85937-326-7	£9.99
Leeds (pb)	1-85937-202-3	£9.99	Shropshire Living Memories	1-85937-643-6	£14.99
Leicester (pb)	1-85937-381-x	£9.99	Somerset	1-85937-153-1	£14.99
Leicestershire & Rutland Living Memories	1-85937-500-6	£12.99	South Devon Coast	1-85937-107-8	£14.99
Leicestershire (pb)	1-85937-185-x	£9.99	South Devon Living Memories (pb)	1-85937-609-6	£9.99
Lighthouses	1-85937-257-0	£9.99	South East London (pb)	1-85937-263-5	£9.99
Lincoln (pb)	1-85937-380-1	£9.99	South Somerset	1-85937-318-6	£14.99
Lincolnshire (pb)	1-85937-433-6	£9.99	South Wales	1-85937-519-7	£14.99
Liverpool and Merseyside (pb)	1-85937-234-1	£9.99	Southampton (pb)	1-85937-427-1	£9.99
London (pb)	1-85937-183-3	£9.99	Southend (pb)	1-85937-313-5	£9.99
London Living Memories	1-85937-454-9	£14.99	Southport (pb)	1-85937-425-5	£9.99
Ludlow (pb)	1-85937-176-0	£9.99	St Albans (pb)	1-85937-341-0	£9.99
Luton (pb)	1-85937-235-x	£9.99	St Ives (pb)	1-85937-415-8	£9.99
Maidenhead (pb)	1-85937-339-9	£9.99	Stafford Living Memories (pb)	1-85937-503-0	£9.99
Maidstone (pb)	1-85937-391-7	£9.99	Staffordshire (pb)	1-85937-308-9	£9.99
Manchester (pb)	1-85937-198-1	£9.99	Stourbridge (pb)	1-85937-530-8	£9.99
Marlborough (pb)	1-85937-336-4	£9.99	Stratford upon Avon (pb)	1-85937-388-7	£9.99
Middlesex	1-85937-158-2	£14.99	Suffolk (pb)	1-85937-221-x	£9.99
Monmouthshire	1-85937-532-4	£14.99	Suffolk Coast (pb)	1-85937-610-x	£9.99
New Forest (pb)	1-85937-390-9	£9.99	Surrey (pb)	1-85937-240-6	£9.99
Newark (pb)	1-85937-366-6	£9.99	Surrey Living Memories	1-85937-328-3	£14.99
Newport, Wales (pb)	1-85937-258-9	£9.99	Sussex (pb)	1-85937-184-1	£9.99
Newquay (pb)	1-85937-421-2	£9.99	Sutton (pb)	1-85937-337-2	£9.99
Norfolk (pb)	1-85937-195-7	£9.99	Swansea (pb)	1-85937-167-1	£9.99
Norfolk Broads	1-85937-486-7	£14.99	Taunton (pb)	1-85937-314-3	£9.99
Norfolk Living Memories (pb)	1-85937-402-6	£9.99	Tees Valley & Cleveland (pb)	1-85937-623-1	£9.99
North Buckinghamshire	1-85937-626-6	£14.99	Teignmouth (pb)	1-85937-370-4	£7.99
North Devon Living Memories	1-85937-261-9	£14.99	Thanet (pb)	1-85937-116-7	£9.99
North Hertfordshire	1-85937-547-2	£14.99	Tiverton (pb)	1-85937-178-7	£9.99
North London (pb)	1-85937-403-4	£9.99	Torbay (pb)	1-85937-597-9	£9.99
North Somerset	1-85937-302-x	£14.99	Truro (pb)	1-85937-598-7	£9.99
North Wales (pb)	1-85937-298-8	£9.99	Victorian & Edwardian Dorset	1-85937-254-6	£14.99
North Yorkshire (pb)	1-85937-236-8	£9.99	Victorian & Edwardian Kent (pb)	1-85937-624-X	£9.99
Northamptonshire Living Memories	1-85937-529-4	£14.99	Victorian & Edwardian Maritime Album (pb)	1-85937-622-3	£9.99
Northamptonshire	1-85937-150-7	£14.99	Victorian and Edwardian Sussex (pb)	1-85937-625-8	£9.99
Northumberland Tyne & Wear (pb)	1-85937-281-3	£9.99	Villages of Devon (pb)	1-85937-293-7	£9.99
Northumberland	1-85937-522-7	£14.99	Villages of Kent (pb)	1-85937-294-5	£9.99
Norwich (pb)	1-85937-194-9	£8.99	Villages of Sussex (pb)	1-85937-295-3	£9.99
Nottingham (pb)	1-85937-324-0	£9.99	Warrington (pb)	1-85937-507-3	£9.99
Nottinghamshire (pb)	1-85937-187-6	£9.99	Warwick (pb)	1-85937-518-9	£9.99
Oxford (pb)	1-85937-411-5	£9.99	Warwickshire (pb)	1-85937-203-1	£9.99
Oxfordshire (pb)	1-85937-430-1	£9.99	Welsh Castles (pb)	1-85937-322-4	£9.99
Oxfordshire Living Memories	1-85937-525-1	£14.99	West Midlands (pb)	1-85937-289-9	£9.99
Paignton (pb)	1-85937-374-7	£7.99	West Sussex (pb)	1-85937-607-x	£9.99
Peak District (pb)	1-85937-280-5	£9.99	West Yorkshire (pb)	1-85937-201-5	£9.99
Pembrokeshire	1-85937-262-7	£14.99	Weston Super Mare (pb)	1-85937-306-2	£9.99
Penzance (pb)	1-85937-595-2	£9.99	Weymouth (pb)	1-85937-209-0	£9.99
Peterborough (pb)	1-85937-219-8	£9.99	Wiltshire (pb)	1-85937-277-5	£9.99
Picturesque Harbours	1-85937-208-2	£14.99	Wiltshire Churches (pb)	1-85937-171-x	£9.99
Piers	1-85937-237-6	£17.99	Wiltshire Living Memories (pb)	1-85937-396-8	£9.99
Plymouth (pb)	1-85937-389-5	£9.99	Winchester (pb)	1-85937-428-x	£9.99
Poole & Sandbanks (pb)	1-85937-251-1	£9.99	Windsor (pb)	1-85937-333-x	£9.99
Preston (pb)	1-85937-212-0	£9.99	Wokingham & Bracknell (pb)	1-85937-329-1	£9.99
Reading (pb)	1-85937-238-4	£9.99	Woodbridge (pb)	1-85937-498-0	£9.99
Redhill to Reigate (pb)	1-85937-596-0	£9.99	Worcester (pb)	1-85937-165-5	£9.99
Ringwood (pb)	1-85937-384-4	£7.99	Worcestershire Living Memories	1-85937-489-1	£14.99
Romford (pb)	1-85937-319-4	£9.99	Worcestershire	1-85937-152-3	£14.99
Royal Tunbridge Wells (pb)	1-85937-504-9	£9.99	York (pb)	1-85937-199-x	£9.99
Salisbury (pb)	1-85937-239-2	£9.99	Yorkshire (pb)	1-85937-186-8	£9.99
Scarborough (pb)	1-85937-379-8	£9.99	Yorkshire Coastal Memories	1-85937-506-5	£14.99
Sevenoaks and Tonbridge (pb)	1-85937-392-5	£9.99	Yorkshire Dales	1-85937-502-2	£14.99
Sheffield & South Yorks (pb)	1-85937-267-8	£9.99	Yorkshire Living Memories (pb)	1-85937-397-6	£9.99

See Frith books on the internet at www.francisfrith.co.uk

FRITH PRODUCTS & SERVICES

Francis Frith would doubtless be pleased to know that the pioneering publishing venture he started in 1860 still continues today. Over a hundred and forty years later, The Francis Frith Collection continues in the same innovative tradition and is now one of the foremost publishers of vintage photographs in the world. Some of the current activities include:

Interior Decoration

Today Frith's photographs can be seen framed and as giant wall murals in thousands of pubs, restaurants, hotels, banks, retail stores and other public buildings throughout the country. In every case they enhance the unique local atmosphere of the places they depict and provide reminders of gentler days in an increasingly busy and frenetic world.

Product Promotions

Frith products are used by many major companies to promote the sales of their own products or to reinforce their own history and heritage. Frith promotions have been used by Hovis bread, Courage beers, Scots Porage Oats, Colman's mustard, Cadbury's foods, Mellow Birds coffee, Dunhill pipe tobacco, Guinness, and Bulmer's Cider.

Genealogy and Family History

As the interest in family history and roots grows world-wide, more and more people are turning to Frith's photographs of Great Britain for images of the towns, villages and streets where their ancestors lived; and, of course, photographs of the churches and chapels where their ancestors were christened, married and buried are an essential part of every genealogy tree and family album.

Frith Products

All Frith photographs are available Framed or just as Mounted Prints and Posters (size 23 x 16 inches). These may be ordered from the address below. From time to time other products - Address Books, Calendars, Table Mats, etc - are available.

The Internet

Already fifty thousand Frith photographs can be viewed and purchased on the internet through the Frith websites and a myriad of partner sites.

For more detailed information on Frith companies and products, look at these sites:

www.francisfrith.co.uk
www.francisfrith.com
(for North American visitors)

See the complete list of Frith Books at:

www.francisfrith.co.uk

This web site is regularly updated with the latest list of publications from the Frith Book Company. If you wish to buy books relating to another part of the country that your local bookshop does not stock, you may purchase on-line.

For further information, trade, or author enquiries please contact us at the address below:
The Francis Frith Collection, Frith's Barn, Teffont, Salisbury, Wiltshire, England SP3 5QP.
Tel: +44 (0)1722 716 376 Fax: +44 (0)1722 716 881   Email: sales@francisfrith.co.uk

See Frith books on the internet at www.francisfrith.co.uk

FREE PRINT OF YOUR CHOICE

Mounted Print
Overall size 14 x 11 inches (355 x 280mm)

Choose any Frith photograph in this book.
Simply complete the Voucher opposite and return it with your remittance for £2.25 (to cover postage and handling) and we will print the photograph of your choice in SEPIA (size 11 x 8 inches) and supply it in a cream mount with a burgundy rule line (overall size 14 x 11 inches).
Please note: photographs with a reference number starting with a "Z" are not Frith photographs and cannot be supplied under this offer.
Offer valid for delivery to one UK address only.

PLUS: Order additional Mounted Prints at HALF PRICE - £7.49 each (normally £14.99)
If you would like to order more Frith prints from this book, possibly as gifts for friends and family, you can buy them at half price (with no additional postage and handling costs).

PLUS: Have your Mounted Prints framed
For an extra £14.95 per print you can have your mounted print(s) framed in an elegant polished wood and gilt moulding, overall size 16 x 13 inches (no additional postage and handling required).

IMPORTANT!

These special prices are only available if you use this form to order . You must use the ORIGINAL VOUCHER on this page (no copies permitted). We can only despatch to one UK address. This offer cannot be combined with any other offer.

Send completed Voucher form to:
The Francis Frith Collection, Frith's Barn, Teffont, Salisbury, Wiltshire SP3 5QP

CHOOSE A PHOTOGRAPH FROM THIS BOOK

Voucher for **FREE** and Reduced Price Frith Prints

Please do not photocopy this voucher. Only the original is valid, so please fill it in, cut it out and return it to us with your order.

Picture ref no	Page no	Qty	Mounted @ £7.49	Framed + £14.95	Total Cost £
		1	Free of charge*	£	£
			£7.49	£	£
			£7.49	£	£
			£7.49	£	£
			£7.49	£	£
			£7.49	£	£

Please allow 28 days for delivery.
Offer available to one UK address only

* Post & handling		£2.25
Total Order Cost		£

Title of this book . . . .

I enclose a cheque/postal order for £ . . . .
made payable to 'The Francis Frith Collection'

OR please debit my Mastercard / Visa / Maestro / Amex card, details below

Card Number

Issue No (Maestro only)   Valid from (Maestro)

Expires   Signature

Name Mr/Mrs/Ms . . . .
Address . . . .
. . . .
. . . .
. . . . Postcode . . . .
Daytime Tel No . . . .
Email . . . .

Valid to 31/12/07

Free Print – see overleaf

Would you like to find out more about Francis Frith?

We have recently recruited some entertaining speakers who are happy to visit local groups, clubs and societies to give an illustrated talk documenting Frith's travels and photographs. If you are a member of such a group and are interested in hosting a presentation, we would love to hear from you.

Our speakers bring with them a small selection of our local town and county books, together with sample prints. They are happy to take orders. A small proportion of the order value is donated to the group who have hosted the presentation. The talks are therefore an excellent way of fundraising for small groups and societies.

Can you help us with information about any of the Frith photographs in this book?

We are gradually compiling an historical record for each of the photographs in the Frith archive. It is always fascinating to find out the names of the people shown in the pictures, as well as insights into the shops, buildings and other features depicted.

If you recognize anyone in the photographs in this book, or if you have information not already included in the author's caption, do let us know. We would love to hear from you, and will try to publish it in future books or articles.

Our production team

Frith books are produced by a small dedicated team at offices in the converted Grade II listed 18th-century barn at Teffont near Salisbury, illustrated above. Most have worked with the Frith Collection for many years. All have in common one quality: they have a passion for the Frith Collection. The team is constantly expanding, but currently includes:

Paul Baron, Phillip Brennan, Jason Buck, John Buck, Ruth Butler, Heather Crisp, David Davies, Louis du Mont, Isobel Hall, Gareth Harris, Lucy Hart, Julian Hight, Peter Horne, James Kinnear, Karen Kinnear, Tina Leary, Stuart Login, David Marsh, Lesley-Ann Millard, Sue Molloy, Glenda Morgan, Wayne Morgan, Sarah Roberts, Kate Rotondetto, Dean Scource, Eliza Sackett, Terence Sackett, Sandra Sampson, Adrian Sanders, Sandra Sanger, Jan Scrivens, Julia Skinner, David Smith, Miles Smith, Lewis Taylor, Shelley Tolcher, Lorraine Tuck, Amanita Wainwright and Ricky Williams.